The Fox in the Moon

Based on a
Peruvian Folk Tale

Retold by Juan Quintana and Michael Ryall
Illustrated by Francisco X. Mora

HAMPTON-BROWN BOOKS

MANY CULTURES, MANY LANGUAGES . . . MANY POSSIBILITIES™

A long, long time ago, when animals could
still talk, Fox and Mole were the best of friends.
On full-moon nights, they both liked to sit outside
in the moonlight. They would often stay up late into
the night, telling stories and sharing dreams.

ne night, Fox told Mole his craziest dream of all:
he wanted to go to the moon.

Mole didn't care one bit about going to the moon.
All he cared about was eating worms—big, fat, juicy
worms. He dreamed about having worms for breakfast,
lunch, and dinner. Worms were the first thing he thought
about when he woke up and the last thing he thought
about before going to sleep.

"▦ wish I could go to the moon," said Fox. "What a wonderful place it must be. Hey! I've got an idea. Will you come with me, Mole?"

Mole thought that was the craziest idea he had ever heard. "The moon is so high," he said. "It's impossible."

"But I have a plan," said Fox. "We'll wait for the crescent moon. Then we can tie a very long rope to the moon and climb up the rope—it will be easy!"

ole just frowned.

"Did I tell you there are worms on the moon?" asked Fox.

Mole's eyes became big and round. "Worms?"

"Yes! There are thousands of worms everywhere. You can have worms for breakfast, lunch, and dinner if you want."

"And dessert, too?" asked Mole.

"You can have as many as you want," Fox answered.

And so Fox convinced Mole to go with him to the moon.

The next night, they started making the longest rope in the world.

They worked together night . . .

after night . . .

after night . . .

until they finished the rope. Then, they waited for the crescent moon to appear.

inally, the moon was just the right shape.

Fox and Mole went to see Bear in his cave.

"Dear Bear," they said, "you are the best tree-climber of all. Please, oh please, climb to the top of the highest tree and tie this rope around the moon."

Bear said he would try.

Bear climbed up, up, and up to the top of the highest tree. When he got to the top, he stood on tip-toe and s-t-r-e-t-c-h-e-d as far as he could. But he couldn't reach the moon. It was too high.

So, Fox and Mole asked Llama for help.

"Dear Llama, you are the best mountain-climber of all. Please, oh please, climb to the top of the highest mountain and tie this rope around the moon."

Llama said she would try.

llama climbed up, up, and up to the top of the highest mountain. When she got to the top, she went to the edge of the mountain and s-t-r-e-t-c-h-e-d her neck as far as she could. But she couldn't reach the moon. It was too high.

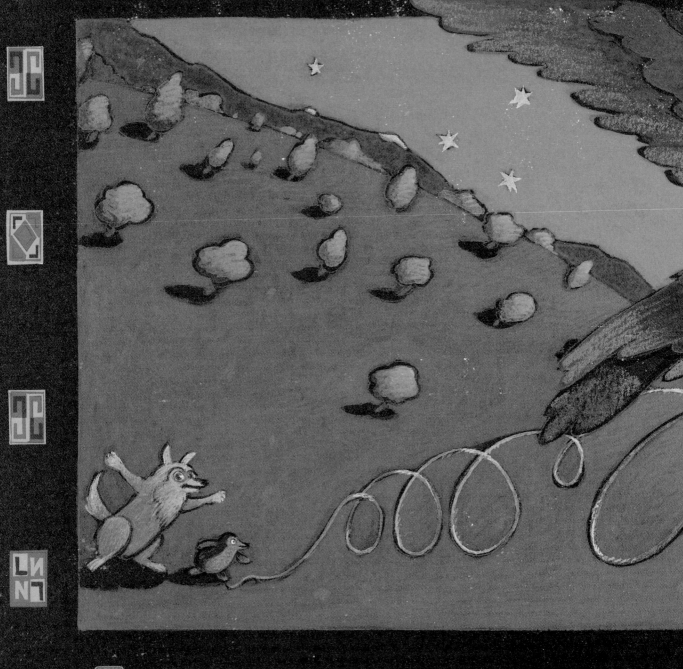

So, Fox and Mole asked Condor for help.

"Dear Condor, you can fly higher than anybody else. Please, oh please, fly as high as you can and tie this rope around the moon."

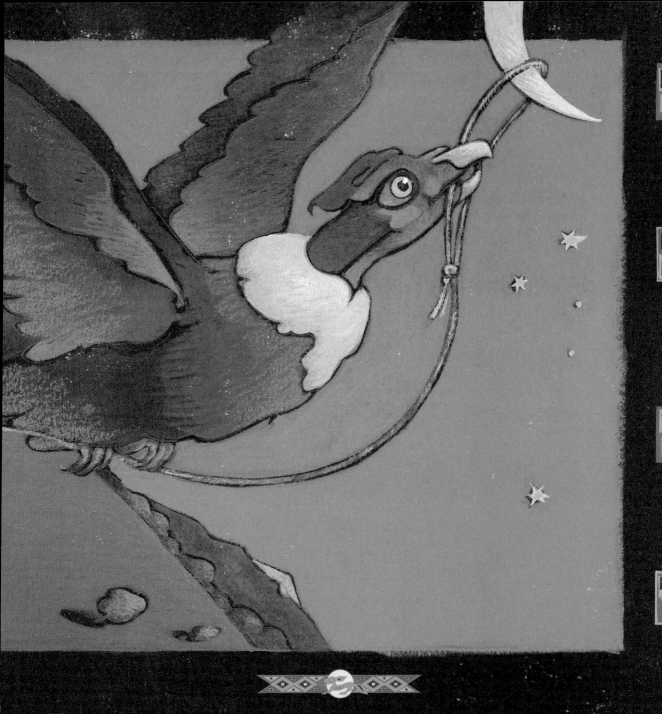

ondor grabbed the rope with his beak and flew high into the sky. Up, up, and up he flew in great big circles, each circle higher than the last. When he flew as high as he could, he s-t-r-e-t-c-h-e-d his neck and—at last!—he tied the rope around the moon.

"ooray!" shouted Mole.

"Thank you, Condor!" shouted Fox. He tied the other end of the rope to a tree and immediately started to climb.

"Come on, Mole," Fox yelled. "It's moon time!"

ole watched Fox climb the rope. The moon was so high! He closed his eyes and thought about all the worms on the moon. Then he opened his eyes and very slowly, very carefully, he started to climb up the rope.

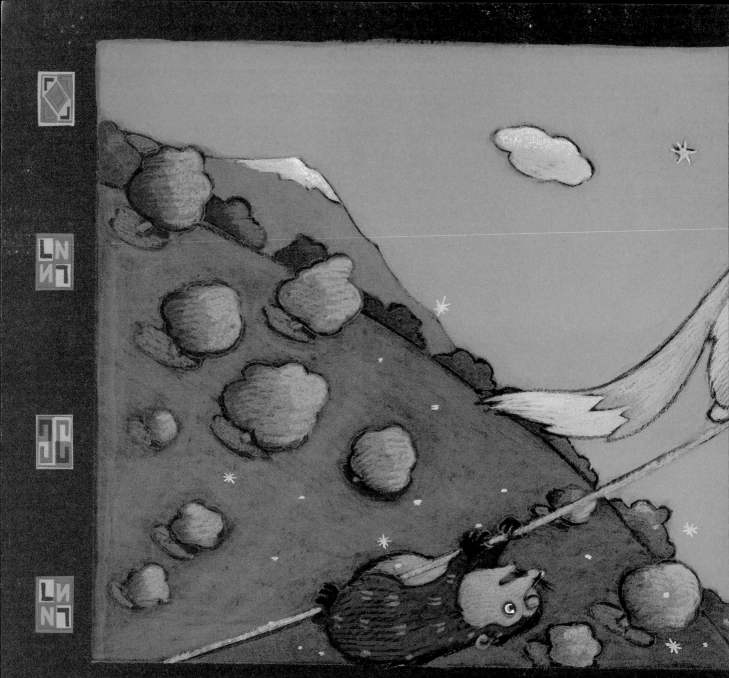

p, up, and up they climbed, higher than the highest trees.

"Oh! I get scared when I look down! Hey, Fox," shouted Mole. "Are we almost there?"

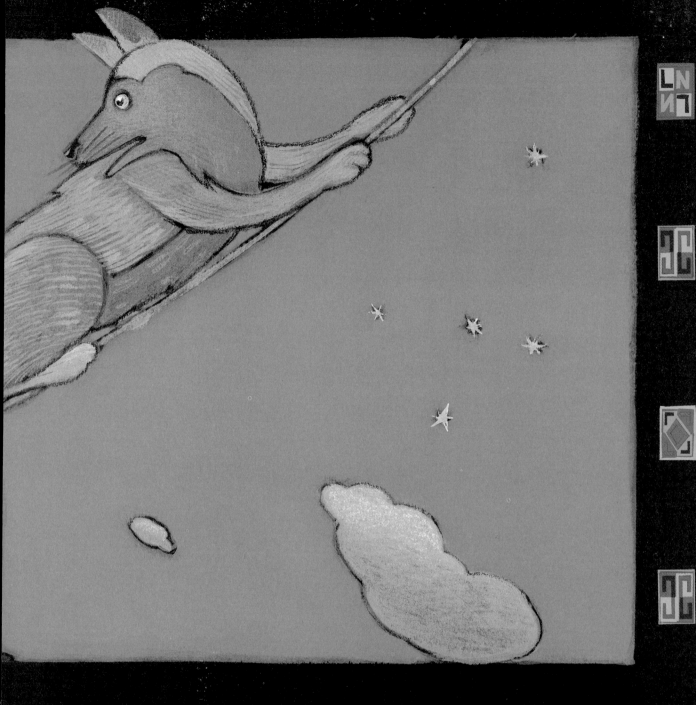

"Just a little bit higher, Mole," replied Fox. "Think of the worms. And don't look down, whatever you do!"

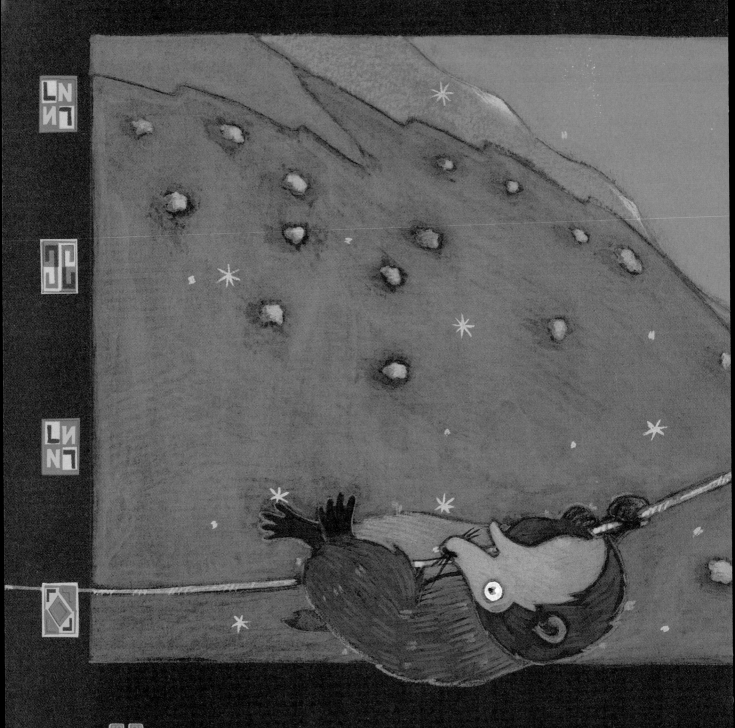

p, up, and up they climbed, higher than the highest mountains.

"Hey, Fox," shouted Mole again. "Are we almost there? It's cold up here and I get dizzy every time I look down."

"We're almost there, Mole!" shouted Fox. "Just keep thinking about the worms. And remember, don't look down!"

p, up, and up they climbed,
higher than the highest cloud.
Then Mole looked down. He
got so dizzy that he let go
of the rope and fell

down,

down,

down,

to the ground.

He hit the Earth so hard that he went deep into the ground. Mole was very embarrassed and wanted to hide. That's why Mole still lives underground to this day.

nd Fox? Fox climbed all the way to the moon and lived there happily for the rest of his life. And in Peru, where this story comes from, people say that on a clear night you can see the shape of a fox in the moon.

The Story Behind the Story

Is there really a fox on the moon?
People in Peru say there is.

People in the
United States say
there is a man
in the moon.

People in Mexico, Korea, and
Japan say there is a rabbit.

People in China say
there is a toad.

But there's not really a fox, or a man, or a rabbit, or a toad in the moon. What's *really* there?

Fine gray dust, sand, pebbles, and boulders are on the moon. These are all different forms of rocks. In fact, the moon itself is just one huge, dry rock.

There are rocks . . .

There are also thousands of craters all over the moon. Rocks called *meteors* fly through space all the time. When they hit the moon, they make dents, or craters. Some craters are bigger than your school, and some are smaller than your fingertip. Did you know there are craters on Earth, too?

. . . and craters.

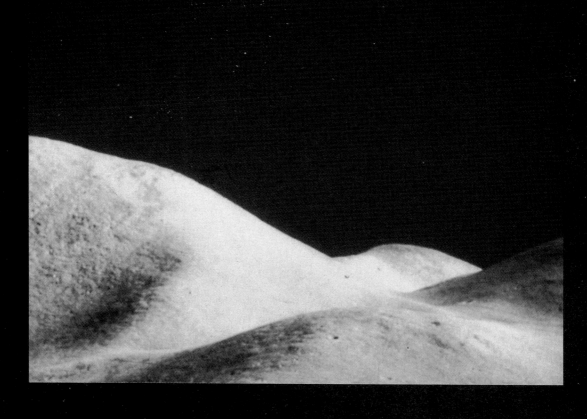

When you look at the moon, the brighter places are mostly mountains and hills. The darker places are low areas between two mountains, or valleys. There are hills, mountains, and valleys on the moon just like on Earth.

There are mountains and valleys . . .

The dark areas on the moon are smooth and flat, like the inside of a crater. In fact, some of them *are* craters. Others were formed long ago by hot, molten rock that flowed out of the moon and covered large areas. A long time ago, people thought these were seas full of water. Now we know that is not true.

. . . and "seas."

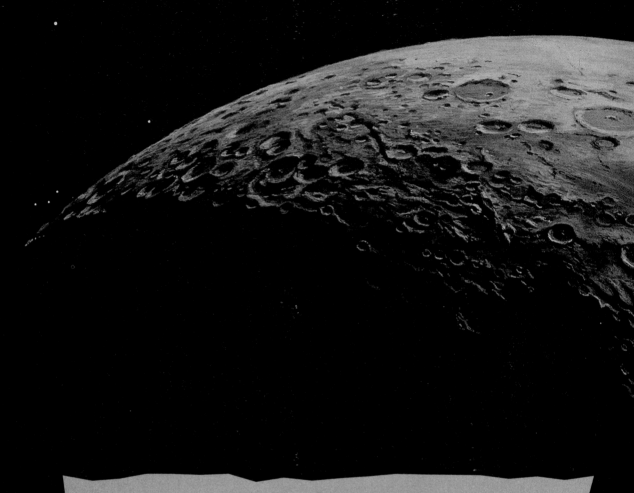

The Earth has air everywhere, but the moon has no air. Air carries sound and water, and it makes our sky blue. Because there is no air on the moon, the sky is always black and it is completely quiet. Without air, temperatures get very hot during the day (200°F or hotter!) and very cold at night (-200°F.)

But there is no air . . .

Nothing can live on the moon.
Without air, there can be no water.
Without water, there can be no plants or animals. People need air,
water, plants, and animals to live, so we cannot live there, either,
unless we bring our own air and water.

. . . or water.

But there *are* footprints on the moon. Astronauts from Earth left footprints, a U.S. flag, a falcon feather, a four-leaf clover, and a sign that says:

HERE MEN FROM THE PLANET EARTH
FIRST SET FOOT UPON THE MOON
JULY 1969, A.D.
WE CAME IN PEACE FOR ALL MANKIND.

What would *you* take to the moon?